Papaya Fantasia

First published 2018 by The Hedgehog Poetry Press

Published in the UK by
The Hedgehog Poetry Press
Coppack House, 5
Churchill Avenue
Clevedon
BS21 6QW

www.hedgehogpress.co.uk

ISBN: 978-1-9996402-5-5

A CIP Catalogue record for this book is available from the British Library.

Acknowledgments
Grateful acknowledgement is made to the editors of the following publications in which some of these poems first appeared, sometimes in different forms:

Prole, Orbis, Envoi, The Journal, Open Mouse, Quintet and Other Poets (Cinnamon Press), *Lost Voices* (Liquorice Fish Books), *Wheel of the Stars* (Ver Poets), *John Cotton's Ten Liners 2017* (Ver Poets), *The Ver Prize 2017 Anthology* and *Taking Notes* (Poetry Space).

Return of the Spider Mother was shortlisted for the Montreal International Poetry Prize 2017. *Your Call is Important to Us* won the Humour Prize in the Southport Writer's Circle Poetry Competition 2018.

My thanks also to Eileen Carney Hulme for pointing me in the direction of the wonderful world of Hedgehog, Mary Smith and my friends at Dumfries Writers who are always so encouraging about my poetry (and especially JoAnne McKay for the workshop that got me started on Papaya Fantasia), John Priestley at Kirkcudbright Poetry Group for the unrelenting "homework", John and Jean Mantle at the U3A Poetry Group for the chance to air new work, Patricia McKaw for enlivening my engagement with poetry, my unpaid publicist, Rob Waite, and last but not least, the High Hedgehog himself, Mark Davidson.

Contents:

Papaya Fantasia

by

David Mark Williams

For Val and Meredith

TICKET

I asked the man behind the glass: "Is it possible to get a ticket all the way to the interior?"

"Well, anything is possible," he replied. "Moreover, from where I'm sitting you look to me like someone up to his knees in possibilities. Single or return?"

YOUR CALL IS IMPORTANT TO US

Please be aware
all our operators are busy right now
but as you wait, enjoy your breath,
be lulled by Vivaldi. Rest assured,
it's all happening beautifully,
the time will go in a heartbeat.

Once you're connected
one of our colleagues will lead you to a life
where nothing happens,
a lovely limbo with a view.

Your call is important to us,
the potted plant at your side
which we shall never refer to
but sense the delicate fronds of,
is important to us also,
and the rain falling heavily through trees,
leaves pressed against the glass,
all this is important too.

We think it would please you to know
your conversation may be recorded
for training purposes and possibly beamed
to every corner of the galaxy.

We hope you are seated comfortably
or even better standing up straight
to give your voice the weight of someone
who knows what they're about.

The slow leak in your life jacket,
that knocking in your pipes,
will be of no consequence,
figure in no equation.

You will be connected as soon as possible.
Thank you for your continued patience.

BIG RED OUTING

I did not take the usual path today
to where I was expected,
hopping instead on the first big red bus
to come my way, a Routemaster storming down the road
like a thumping jukebox of a bygone era.
I sat on the top deck looking down
and with every tune that came into my head
I sang along and as I rode
the streets were blessed with rock and roll
and stalls of polished fruit.
And so uplifted, I fell into conversation
with two ladies fair, like me adrift,
one with blazing hair and a necklace of pearls,
the other delicate as an orchid.
They told me they had noted my efforts
to expand the boundaries of the day
and of this most firmly they approved.
So I continued in their company, all the way
to that Happy Hour, our mystery terminus,
where with a drum roll and a circus shazam,
our glorious bus burst through a paper wall,
leaving a jagged corona of crimson, and the driver said:
Now that's what I call making an entrance.
Oh, let's all stop here and have fun.
That's okay with us, we replied.
Then it was cocktails for the ladies, for me a foaming stein
as we came to the conclusion
this really was the end of the line.

THE MEMORY HOUSE

Think of it as a house
she told me at the beginning.
To go there, I have to close my eyes.
We build it week by week.
I have to do this on my own.
She cannot go with me.
Some of the windows are lit,
but most of the house is in darkness.
There is a high fence to climb over,
warning signs to ignore. Once inside,
I feel my way blind along the corridors
and try the handle of every door.
It is not my father's house
but he is there with his anger
set off again. I saw him once through glass
but he could not touch me.
Sometimes my brother comes around.
I follow in the glow of all he knows.
He carries a bag fat with memories.
Was it your brother gave you these?
Perhaps I should speak to him.
The hour we keep is all we have together.
I bring her what I have found,
fixed in words on sheets of paper
scattered over the table between us.
What is memory and what is a dream
we cannot know for sure.
Be wary of dreams, she says.
They don't lie but they are not the truth.
Remember, what is unreal
cannot be undone. I nod my head
to show I've understood.

WHEN I COULD FLY

What wings I had then.
They never failed me.
To make myself light was easy,
the air my haven
when the world shouted,
when it coiled with threat,
the giant words of billboards booming,
the hiss and clatter of milk floats,
the brazen boys kicking hell
out of a football,
hollering to the skies.
In every field a bull was waiting,
biding its ire,
for the lesson I had to learn.
Under the water of the least pool,
the drowned ones
shouted mutely, reaching up
to pull me down.
None of them got close enough.
I was a bird flying over
the poster bright town.
The day I dropped
from the top of the stairs
I saw my father look up,
too late he thought,
opening his arms anyway.
He did not need to fear.
I missed the axe edge
of each stone step
gliding safely
to land with a slap on the mat.

That moment would shine
for my father ever after
but how soon it would be
when I sat on the stairs
of the empty house, alone,
the angel of demolition
waiting outside,
holding my broken wings.

SCHOOL OF LITTLE BIRDS

We all know the head of the headmistress
unscrews like a light bulb.
She takes it off when she's done her rounds.
It's such a weight to carry.
She props it up on the big desk
she sits behind to steer us through the day,
her body stiff as a dress
on a dress maker's doll, stick legs on castors
ready to be wheeled away.
The head does not rest with its hair
of white chalk, the eyes keep busy,
miss nothing, an ear always cocked
for the next little bird hovering to sing
on her windowsill. We see the head every day,
back on her shoulders, gliding along
the empty corridor where darkness slouches.
One look from her will stop the bleeding
of a finger. She will suffer no tears.
Whatever's broken will mend.
She runs the school so it stays where it is,
beautifully seated and still, never giddy
and tugging to be up in the sky.
Where would her birds be then,
blown about, losing their way?
When she speaks to you,
you must look her in the eyes.
A child who cannot look you in the face
has something to hide.
Don't be surprised she knows everything you do.

A little bird told her so. She knows
who's been screaming blue murder,
who's been showing off, who told a fib.
Oh, we are all her little birds,
piping the truth, the whole truth
and nothing but the truth.

BUS O' BEDLAM

Well here she is, Queen of us all,
smacked in the head with a daffodil,
her eyes coins of sunshine gleaming new-minted.

She's a case, she's a singing bird,
you can't shut her up, flushed with springtime,
arms full of flowers to strew down the aisle.

She sets us off. We're hounds unleashed,
baying like bodies bathed in moonlight.
She plays the tune we long to hear,
round after round as we climb to the skies.

The day's dusted to gold, we dance as we spin,
blessed by the truth that's a flame in the mouth.

With a hole in your soul, rags for clothes,
nourishment may be found all the same.
In desert places it falls like snow.
Our daily bread melts on the tongue.

There's a choir in the engine speeds us uphill.
We rattle on the spine of a giant asleep,
silent as stone until it's time to blunder around
on a pantomime stage unlocking pandemonium.

The driver's a drummer tranced at the wheel.
He'll drum us to Fechan, the gates of paradise
then back to where it all began
in the middle of Noman's Land.

It's been a long dream but now
we're ready to rise on a slow handclap,
waking with wonder to a clatter of wings,
scarecrows shaking, an audience of crows.

Pass the bottle round and take a long sip
put fire in your belly, a skip in your step
shaky legs will find their dancing feet
but don't wander too far. This bus won't wait.

No need to declare what we're riding on.
All heads turn as we go by.
Climb aboard and fill your boots!
Everyone's welcome no matter how blessed.

Tom is our guide, Tom's our man
rolling his eyes, crossing his heart,
here to tell us all he's seen.
Go find him a Rhymer who'll set it all down
in lines that will live after we're gone.

On the Bus o' Bedlam, on the edge of reason
we bang through the air, need no asylum,
for what fills our heads can be found everywhere.

INSIDE THE CLOUD ACADEMY

Imagination is not required here. There is no room
for dreamers at The Cloud Academy.
You have chosen the life of clouds,
by that we mean the proper study of them.
Clouds appear to be shifting and elusive.
Their taxonomy is not. Blessed with knowledge,
an observant eye, it is always possible for clouds
to be properly classified. You must grapple
with identification as if it were the rules
of grammar, and not be overwhelmed
by the species that adhere to genera,
all the shifting varieties. You may be inspired
by the exploits of our wonderful fighter pilots,
contrail makers, bending weather in their wake
but you have no entry to that reckless realm.
From the ground is enough to claim
each cloud by name, and on days when the sky
cannot be usefully deciphered, turn to your Cloud Atlases.
There you will find all you need to know.
To live in the domain of clouds is to watch
thoughts form and not be possessed by them.
Duly note each one then let it go,
returning to what matters, your studies.
Sing the cloud song every morning
and when the day is over, sing again.
Together chant the names of the clouds.
Those who only move their mouths, saying nothing,
will be found out. Inside The Cloud Academy
is to be cocooned, radiantly arrested.
These are your golden years. Make the most of them.
Be clear what awaits you when you leave.

Back among people who do not speak the language of clouds,
crowds of blue sky devotees,
you will be an outsider. Never forget a cloudless sky
is but another version of the void.
Look at it for too long and rest assured
you will lose your way, you will fade.

GIVING IT LARGE FROM THE BACK OF THE BUS

Flaunting their stripes,
they wasp the air.

Recklessly dosed on whatever,
how well they'd do
under a jackass panjandrum
as feckless as they are.
Whatever line was spun
they'd follow and spin too,
lobbing news at everyone
to fight faux with faux.

The sticky orange fizz of them
goes a long way.
They make the hole in the doughnut
bigger by the minute,
and of this bus a zoo.

Don't get your hopes up.
They're not about to disembark
anytime soon.

Nothing to say, they say it louder,
caroming the bona fide dada,
spraying sneer and bray.

Is there a dreamer on board
they might entrance,
who celebrates all God's
finely judged spikes of annoyance,
who sees wasps as golden fliers,
drops of sunlight?

Not you who'd bat them away,
sour face scowling,
who would have guessed
you'd turn out such a groan
so long ago it was,
laughing your head off on the back seat
all the way home.

THE PENCIL FACTORY

My father works in the pencil factory
like most of the fathers in our town.

I watch him set off every morning
on the immaculate bike he's so proud of,
polychromatic red frame, white walled tyres.

He comes home clean as a whistle
and every time reads the disappointment in my eyes
that he's never dusky with graphite.

Contrary to popular belief, he tells me,
Making pencils is not a dirty business.
We work in laboratory conditions.

My father has been at pains several times
to explain to me how pencils are made
but he might as well talk to a brick wall
for all that I can follow what he says.

Our house is full of pencils,
sadly the only perk of the job.

With all the colours at my disposal,
I choose only black, a soft lead.
I draw in my room with the light off.
It's how the night unravels
when you look at it for long enough.

My father hopes I will follow in his footsteps.
How can I tell him the pencil factory
is not for me? When I inherit his bike
I'll ride it with an abandon that will mystify
and sadden him, leave it broken, beyond repair.

NOMAN MAKES A COMEBACK

Went out and stayed out
for a long time, oh a long time,
more than a body can account for.

Where I was unknown,
lost to all the world's monitoring,
no home to call my own,
the most bed I had a ditch.

I rode the air as the sea,
all ears for the babble of what was being uttered
in my head and on the wind.

I gorged on sun so much
it leaked from my skin but I was golden
deep inside ever after and to the present day.

When I came back
no-one understood a word I spoke.
Who broadcasts the truth unadulterated
is not required among the upright purveyors
of opinion, the plausible influencers, I learned.

A phone to my ear would've made
me look right in the world but I can only
stand out now in the street
and speak as a prophet should

for I am lit forever and forever, returned
to all my senses, and can't be silenced,
my name sprayed in high white letters
bridging the thoroughfares of what's your hurry.

THE A24 VAUDEVILLIAN

The pains he takes for these matinees,
centre stage in his very own little theatre
at the side of the carriageway,

head to foot in spotless white,
soft shoes, kid gloves, straw boater.

He should command a better audience
but he's dying a death out here, ghastly in greasepaint.
Daylight is so unforgiving.

His public, already seated, the ones who stare,
moth faces peering from dark windows, are gone in seconds.

Some doubt he's real, a waxwork figure
conjured to life, an automaton set going
in a programme of exquisite slowness.

Only small children want to stop
and see the show, the answer always no.

Heckled by the roar of engines,
the air around him knocked sideways,
he embraces silence, shaping and rocking it with his cane,

then breaking off to verify with splayed hands
the walls of his glass prison.

A trouper, a true artiste, he is unstoppable,
seguing into the evening performance,

car headlights twirling through crash barriers,
and up in the gods, a few attentive stars,
a vacant moon beaming bravo.

TV FOR THE DEAD

All the repeats don't bother them,
there's something new to notice each time,
something they missed before or have forgotten,

a fleet of clouds racing over a blue sky,
a sharp intake of breath, and that business
when the mouths connect and the music surges.

As for what there is to buy with a card,
all there is to fill a house, to adorn a neck or wrist,
it makes no sense but they watch it anyway.

Light from the TV plays in their empty eyes,
spills and flickers on the polished floor.

What they wanted to say to us they have forgotten,
as we rattle on with our little balloons
of speech popping up unchecked.

They hear birdsong, the trickling of a water feature,
the hum of a household appliance.

All walls are glass. They see through our skin
the bloom of neurons, bones gleaming like milk,
the molten traces of food sliding through us.

They watch us all the time. Nothing is too ordinary:
washing dishes, mopping a floor,

and how every night we die,
the black wings of our dreams beating on white screens.

They love us but stay where they are.
Nothing would induce them to return.

PAPAYA FANTASIA

as if papaya could move
as if papaya could sing

Papaya will show you how,
how to dance sitting down,
singing like a vendor swaying up the street.

Eat light and become papaya,
roll glutted with sunshine,
curved for the slow dance in a terracotta glow.

Make a fiery entrance, burst through paper wall,
a drum roll here we are,
a bright brass interruption, centre stage silhouette.

Spit bitter black seeds, strike out and swing,
fling firecrackers down, snapping demons at your feet.

Papaya will show you how
how to dance with nothing at all
but slow smooth curves, voluptuous ease,

easy as a breeze, honey light of dawn,
juice of morning to fill you up.

So shake each minute bright as carnival
preen and shimmy and slide,
down to the dregs of your cup,

down to the last drop of all you've got
papaya will show you how.

AN ANGRY MAN RUNNING AWAY WHILE SHOUTING AT A SMALL GROUP OF PEOPLE

His bark has no bite,

setting off the merest flutter of bemusement
through that flock of flamingos
he's berating, their lovely plumage unruffled.

So huppa, huppa, little man, on your bike,
a flea in the ear for your pains.
Keep those fine pins pumping.

Small wonder his teeth are serrated
with rage, never to be more than this,
a brief distraction at best.

Such a shame his legs have their own ideas
of where they want to be, tripping like a Lipizzaner
over a surface flat as paper,

drawn on a trajectory of fine lines and arrows
all pointing in the same direction.

Who he was they'll never know and don't much care.
Gone so fast into the apricot wash of evening
he's already no more than a dot.

LIVING WITH THE ICE QUEEN

When we have ice in our veins,
nothing can touch us. We are restored to life.
But always this fear of things melting away:
the fine statues we carve from ice.

Wherever we go, we pack a suitcase of winter.
We live easier when the days are abridged.

Darkness is kind to our skin.
Frost grows through the lost hours,
diamonds sparking the ground that our long cloaks sweep.

We go out every night
driven by cold calculations.

Morning waits like a shop doorway where we shiver
not from the cold but with needs so finely calibrated
we watch them blow away
in grains of powdered snow.

No matter how fallen, she is still the queen
of this white domain.
Sometimes I think her kiss would fix me
though we never kiss.

We share a single room in a white palace,
a mattress of hard snow,
where we lie side by side, until the ceiling rolls away
and we behold a sky studded with stars of ice.

We're happy now everything is glued in place again,
water and trees, the white fields,
the sky cleaned of birds, the way she wishes it to be.

MURDERING *YESTERDAY*

Once inside our slow train,
he wastes no time striking up,
a ukulele in his hand,
mouth working like a Manga gash.

Of all the songs to sing this is the one
most worthy of his signature,
a jaunty deadpan remix
that needs no finessing.

He should be pushing a trolley
of light snacks and refreshments
down the aisle, primed to catch an eye,
a proffered hand.
Impervious to disappointment,
he's no option but to try.

For he would Pied Piper us all
to follow in his wake, marvel
at every desecration
upon the altar of reverence,
past the back yards of terraces,
stuck on this stuttering train,

a theatre at the end of a pier
the sea slapping and thumping below,
and on the stage a lone entertainer
doing his best to wow a sparse audience
who have found themselves there
as if in observance of a bye law.

SHOOTING GALLERY

Look where we've landed.
Pluto's a grand place to be,
a dark planet, a rat hole house.

The walls are frescoes of squirted blood
and aerosol can ravings,
of weeping and blistered plaster.

Shoot me, shoot me, shouts a voice
from inside a black box.

We're easy targets,
all in a row, on the nod, fixed as terracotta,
eyes of glass in the blade of a sunbeam.

The floor's a mess of dropped rigs.
Pluto's got us now, got us for good,
cranked to paradise, burned to the ground,

and listen to this, all the time
flocks of children flit in and out
chasing each other, playing their death games.

To them we're only furniture.
They see no more than they've seen before,
fearless as sparrows, safe as a charm.

Now the word is going round:
someone gave up the ghost today,
made an exit you could almost see,

like a rocket rising into the sweet whatever.
The body's gone. It's been put out in the street.

Remember you said, where there's thunder
there's buckets of rain. Shot down, we get up again.
We know the cost, done the calculation.

Beyond us, there's the dream, the difficult heaven,
the hope we'll chase tomorrow,
stripped of any armour, washed clean.

NIGHT SHIFT AT THE POEM FACTORY

You sleepwalk through it,
missing the compensations of day:
the rattle of the tea trolley,
the odd spell of sunshine.
It's a long shift with a skeleton crew.
You're caught in a dream,
one you're awake to.
Your mind's not on the job.
There's poems ticking away
inside you coiled to explode,
to blow up in your face.
Don't waste your time.
If you can't please the janitors of the word
then what's the point. You're going nowhere.
You've been told often enough:
what you do, think of it as wallpaper,
the beauty of repetition,
without a blemish or obvious flaw.
People crave what's neat,
nothing too deep. They need
something they can identify with.
Stick to the tolerances and you'll be fine.
Stay inside the box, don't be tempted
by fanciful notions or try to finesse
what's perfect as it is.
Keep this up and one day
who knows, it'll be your name
at the top of the list.
But you say it's never going to happen.

You're set on doing the unthinkable,
stop what you're about,
down tools and walk out into the night,
let the ghost in the machine go free,
the poor monster,
gliding by the fields of moonlight,
longing to crawl between the stalks
of whatever's growing there.
You'll do it one day there's no doubt.
You won't be able to stop yourself.
No matter how many times you're told
this machine's your bread and butter,
you know it's not enough.

NOMAN NEEDS TO BEG

I had a house of good stone,
now it's a ruin.
I had money rolling in,
now nothing's accruing.
I had the love of a woman
but it's long over.
I had the promise of heaven
but I won't get there.
I should have taken more care
with the direction I was going.
I should have paid more heed
to the seeds I was sowing.
And I don't know how to beg
but I'm begging.
In the middle of the street, I am begging.
On my one good leg,
mad as a mating heron,
I am begging.
And you can keep your hair on
while I'm begging.
In a pool of my remorse, I am begging
a pool of bitter tears,
I am begging.
For a cup of sweet tea
for my train fare home,
for a foot in the door,
for a place to call my own,
fizzing like a frenzied fly
with one eye on the sky
in my hand a red rose
no one cares to buy

Angry as a bull, I am begging
in a red rag rage
I am begging.
And I'm waiting for the handcart
to take me from here,
and I don't know how to beg
but I'm begging.

THE FLAT EARTH VIEWPOINT

I do not believe the moon, the sphere lie,
the round world conspiracy.

I've flown. I've seen how it is.
I've looked down. The sea, the fields:

how it rolls away flat to the horizon.
Trust the evidence of your senses.

How could you doubt it levels out,
the beauty of everything held in place?

Don't blind me with facts and figures.
If we spin at all, we spin on a plate.

SHARING THE CLOUD ROOM

Missy doesn't mind her music muddy.
It all sounds good to her.
And nothing will make us say goodbye
Now the cloud room is ours to share.

Missy doesn't mind her music muddy,
muffled through old sock speakers.
She sings along with every track,
lyrics mangled, blackbird sweet.

Missy's got my back and I have hers,
this new life keeps us neat.
We're as close to the sky as we would wish for.
We have the clouds and mixtapes,
a dazzling city spread below:

at night it's a lit diorama, siren webs
tracing chasms through the crowded streets.

When we go out, we put on long overcoats
so no-one can see our feet skimming over the ground,
our bones too light to hold us down.

We don't go far, stop at the crossing,
catch the street dancers pivot on pavements
so happy they want to leap
into the road and stop the cars.

When our music's in ribbons
spilled from the spool it's okay.
Let the battery die, we'll stare it down
to the last glimmer in this space among the clouds
smoothed to linen by the moon,
our anchored room secure as the stars.

THE SHIT WAGON

Always a shit wagon
and someone to push it.
Always a shit wagon
under a sweet shitless sky.

No matter how slick the system,
how tight the controls.
Always a demand.
Always a guaranteed need.

Discard your broken furniture.
Bring out your dead.
Give us your shit parcels fat as pigeons
caught on razor wire.

The rattled anthem,
the rumbling of tumbrils,
clatter of plague cart over cobblestones,
dreams of jamroll, always tomorrow,

and when the knockback comes
know how to pass the time.
Sleep your sentence.
Always the shit wagon coming round.

Listen, it's a long story.
Sometimes there's nowhere left to run,
nothing to do but face it,
naked, in the darkness,

in this locked space,
come the morning,
come Armageddon, you'll be
pushing that wagon.

THE LONG WAVE BROADCAST

From the blue and white radio,
my father is speaking,

from the room below, his voice muffled,
to anyone who will listen.

He is hundreds of miles away
broadcasting from a tiny country in Europe,

sound waves pulsing in white ripples
from a radio mast on top of a hill,

over an oil black sea, through squalls of static,
creaking beams and hawsers,

my hand on the scalloped tuner
steering him back.

What he is trying to say, I cannot make out.
Only the sound of his voice,

rising and falling, that won't stop
until this wide awake baby in my arms falls asleep,

fading to nothing as the eyes close.

THE SLUG ROOM

It's their room now,
these damp walls of collapsed plaster,
stripped down, cold as a crypt.

They have made a maze
of lunar trails, tracks of glistening rime,
from their obdurate roaming.

The dark ellipses proliferate,
hump backed islands,
lenticular clouds on a swept sky.

They roll over the waves they create,
hauling their keels behind them.

Their antennae swivel and probe,
sensing light, sniffing the air.

What draws them in we do not know.

There's nothing for them here
except the spores damp and decay emit
or the dead bodies of their own kind.

Some will sleep through the winter,
others make an autumn death.

We seal up cracks but they still appear.

Salt would see them off soon enough.
We'd watch them rear up as if on fire,
but we let them be, keep the door shut.

ODOUR OF NEW BABY

Between the bouts of crying,
those spells of peace,
serene with what her skin gave off,

dopamine, a trace of vernix,
pooled in sutures of fontanelle,
spun on the orbit of a mobile.

How it worked upon us, mixed
with our blood, our breath,

that odour, until the day it was gone,
before we knew what it was.

A POSTCARD FROM KENTUCKY

It's propped up on the window sill.
He's only to move his eyes and there it is.
What's written on the back
he doesn't need to hear again.

The horses are frozen at the bend of the track,
the trees flounced with blossom.
He'll go there one day.

Here it's late October and the crack willow,
the name he can't retain,
fills the window, roaring with blown light.

His head's too heavy. He can't stop it
sliding off the pillow.
All food is paper, nothing you'd want in your mouth.
His breath a snarled machine, grinding down.

Though the heart labours hard
it's always ready to spring.
He'll seize any chance, just say the word
and he'll be off, no need to book a car.
He'll make his own way home.

THE LITTLE MOTHER

She's become so small
you wouldn't know her now.
Her smile is so tiny it's invisible.
There she is again,
dragging herself through the town
with its dead shops, the bright pins
of her eyes scanning for dropped coins
to plump out her purse.
Sometimes if she's lucky,
it's folding money she finds.
She has seen the sky dark with bombers,
a city on fire but that was years ago.
All she ever wanted
was a little home to keep clean.
She's got one now all to herself.
She doesn't mind you visiting
but if you bring her furniture
please make sure it's small.

DEATH AND THE MAIDEN

They are inseparable those two.
I've spotted them before
with their distinctive brand of street theatre,

Death always roaring drunk,
wielding a flagon of cider, the maiden demure,
dressed for an office job, white blouse, pencil skirt.

He used to scare her, but not anymore.
She's got used to his funny little ways.

Tonight we're on the same train,
rattling and sparking through the terraced
and tranquilised suburbs.

There's a little crowd around them near the exit.
They all think he's a scream.

He can keep this up for hours,
toasting every good thing that damn well
demands to be toasted.

It'll be his birthday soon, he keeps saying,
there's going to be a party and everyone's invited.

I'm keeping out of the way.
Perhaps he won't notice me
behind my evening paper.

GRIMWALLS BY THE SEA

You lucky people, washed up here,
written out, written off.
You know how it goes, how it works.

What a tableaux you make,
figures in a municipal installation
waiting for a bus that's always late.

Lucky, plucky people,
you don't exist, the grocer's daughter said,
lobbing the free mint julip for others
who had the wherewithal to help themselves.

The Pier Theatre closed down years ago.
You won't see *Oh It's Him Jim* again
to raise a laugh, lift your spirits.

Anesthetised now, nothing bothers you.
The tabloids fume in vain.
If you're longing for a golden cruise
buy a ticket for the lottery.

The town centre's dead beat;
it speaks of bleak, a terminal decline.
The pound stores go out of business,
the charity shops keep their prices slashed.

Count your blessings, your teeth,
the small change in your pockets.
Splash out on another ornament
for a mantelpiece better left bare.

O you lucky, plucky people,
all plucked out, duck down,
stay exactly where you are,
make the most of what you've got
slap by the gravy grey, the tin foil sea.

RETURN OF THE SPIDER MOTHER

After Louise Bourgeois

You don't have to be cloistered
in a darkened room, crouched over a candle,
to summon her. You don't have
to make a scene, smash crockery or draw
any attention to yourself.

Only allow your anxiety to grow,
spiralling out of you in lines
that cover the walls of white corridors,
and outside are skeins of a broken web
caught on a barbed wire fence.

She knows that you need her,
picked up on your distress signal,
her eyes snapping open,
head swivelling on its smooth gears.
You've waited long enough.

Listen out for her spiked heels
clacking over the flagstones towards you.
Be ready to hold out your arms. Together
you'll rise as high as a steeple, steadied
on pincers locked into the pavement cracks.

She will come back. She's on her way,
the good mother, the fierce mother.
With her needle and thread, she'll repair
all that came undone,
the sky, your lacerated heart.

BUDDHA MAN ON THE BEACH

Conspicuous in black trousers
and crisp white shirt
among the early birds working out,

he walks the promenade to the measure
of a slow, deliberate breath.
On the beach he becomes

a seated figure in an orange robe
to face the sun sliding free
of the wooded ridge.

Let me burn, his body says,
let these bones show white as an x-ray.
He offers no target.

There is nothing but the moment
which itself is nothing,
wave upon wave, breath after breath.

When the boat arrives
chugging close to the shore
to jet wash the pebbles, he does not move

and the boatmen do as they always do,
spray either side of him,
leave him there on a long dry line.

BRAMBLE PICKING

After the painting, Bramble Picking II, *by Margot Sandeman*

What has slowed us down we cannot say.
We are turning to statues, our mouths
have been erased, smooth as pebbles.
We're fenced in with bramble shoots,
tendrils uncoiling into the margins
of this soft grey day.

Our arms are stiff as ladles, no good anymore
for scooping up these soft black jewels
that have inked our hands.
What has collapsed in us
that we stand so still, caught in a moment
that might last forever?

Is there a potion we could drink
to bring us back to life?
A shotgun going off somewhere might
rouse us briefly, we'd rise like a flock of rooks,
scarring the quiet sky,
the white flowers at our feet crying out.

FAUX FUR THROW FIRE

The fire is dying down, settled to cherry glow,
knuckle bones of charcoal.

I should attend to it
but there are the kittens to deal with,
the silly creatures.

They want to lie inside its contours
as if it were a crumpled faux fur throw.

How would it look, their fur singed
to needles, scorched imp bodies,
paws of melted wax?

One by one, I pick them up,
put them down out of harm's way
but they keep crawling back
into the smouldering folds.

I can't let them burn
however much they want to.
I'll put them in the larder where it's cool,
keeping watch, smoke rising from their fur,

as dusk settles like a cloud of soot,
darkening the white shelves, the spotless floor.

LOOKING FOR BUSINESS

No moon tonight
to pour its influence over Kings Cross,
no white plate on a sky stripped of clouds,
no whisky glow from latticed windows
to put a shine on cobblestones,
only this aquarium light.
Drizzle has dampened the streets,
mired the pavements.
Rush hour is over but no one's strolling.
She stands against the flow,
wearing a smeared smile that says:
let's all get out of it.
Her burlesque days over
she doesn't cut it in that grimy suit,
those sexless shoes a school girl
might be made to wear,
bare ankles on display.
Her need is running from her nose.
All she has to offer is a question.
Nobody's taken her up yet,
but they will, some fine gentleman
with a penchant for what's broken,
maybe whisk her away
somewhere warm and dry,
place her inside a glowing cage,
but an alleyway will do,
eyes to the sky to feel the rain hit,
get it done. Make it quick.

NOMADE

After Guame Plensa's Nomade at Port Vauban, Antibes

You're almost not here, fading into sky,
ghost of a moon, end of the line,
hunched over bent knees. What's written
under skin shows in shadow
on the ground, fretwork of a code only
those who love you can break.

There you sit inside an endless reverie,
staring out to sea, lost and found
where the gone wash up
among the sleek boats at anchor,
with all the time that remains,
sand through loosened fingers.

Gulls slicing the air, pay them no mind
fixed you'll stay forever, pied
with slashes of azure, racked to bones,
brooding on what was needed
so many times, nothing so sweet
you couldn't say for words.

What shaped your body scattered to babble,
cut to spinning letters, a flock of startled birds,
a net of white wings,

stacked in steel, risen steeple high.
Below you they're looking up,
who've seen through you, not believing their eyes.

NOMAN FINDS THE EXIT

I am talking nobody's listening.
I am walking nobody beside me.
What do I care, that I have no-one.
I've found the exit and I am free

Oh, car owners of this fair city
Pull to the side now and leave your cars.
Join with me, my stout and worthy ones.
It's time to shake off all your cares.

The Queen of England doesn't mind me,
more than happy to give a wave
but the rest of you when I appear
turn up your noses and look away.

I am talking nobody's listening.
I am walking nobody beside me.
What do I care, that I have no-one.
I've found the exit and I am free

In the dead of night you'll hear me creeping
below your window while you're half asleep.
Ignore at your peril my pearls of wisdom.
Crawl from your beds and walk with me.

Do not wait until you are persuaded.
I've found the exit. I've seen the sign.
In these slow shoes, I'll keep shuffling
while I'm on my feet, while I still have time.

I am talking nobody's listening.
I am walking nobody beside me.
What do I care, that I have no-one.
I've found the exit and I am free

DRIVING THE GHOST BUS

My Lady of Sorrows, my last ghost,
all the others long gone,
is weeping, as she always does, inconsolably,
and will leave her seat blotted with tears.

Never could find a good hearted man.
She'll cry a lot more before we reach the end.
She was looking for the train, forgot
it doesn't run anymore.

The line is a fiction, I told her.
The number means nothing.

I'm where I want to be.
It's all I need. The same route every day,
with no deviations allowed.

They say it's a lot of emptiness to lug around
but it's a good machine, a smooth Dart engine,
a glider for my dreams.

One day the whistle will blow
the game will be up, but until it does
I'll keep driving to see it all play out backwards.

A red moon slicing through stripped trees,
dead leaves skittering like mice.

When we're found out,
I'll take off, follow the road wherever it may go,
stay where I am - always between,

my hands resting lightly on the wheel.